THE
BODY
RESET
DIET
SMOOTHIES

 CookNation

THE BODY RESET DIET SMOOTHIES
Smoothies To Power Your Metabolism, Blast Fat, Lose Weight and Shed Pounds

ISBN 978-1-912511-34-1
Cover image under license from Shutterstock

Disclaimer

The content of this book is also available under the
title 'Time To Try...the Body Reset Diet Smoothies'
by CookNation. Except for use in any review, the
reproduction or utilisation of this work in whole or in part
in any form by any electronic, mechanical or other
means, now known or hereafter invented, including
xerography, photocopying and recording, or in any
information storage or retrieval system, is forbidden
without the permission of the publisher.
This book is sold subject to the condition that it shall
not, by way of trade or otherwise, be lent, resold, hired
out or otherwise circulated without the prior consent
of the publisher in any form of binding or cover other
than that in which it is published and without a similar
condition including this condition being imposed on the
subsequent purchaser.
This book is designed to provide information on
smoothies that can be made in conjunction with the
popular Body Reset Diet. Some recipes may contain
nuts or traces of nuts. Those suffering from any allergies
associated with nuts should avoid any recipes
containing nuts or nut based oils.

This information is provided and sold with the knowledge
that the publisher and author do not offer any legal or
other professional advice.
In the case of a need for any such expertise consult with
the appropriate professional.
All the recipes in this book have been tested using the
Nutribullet 600 series blender (large cup) but they can be
adjusted for use with any quality personal blender on the
market.
This book does not contain all information available on
the subject, and other sources of recipes are available.
Every effort has been made to make this book
as accurate as possible. However, there may be
typographical and or content errors. Therefore, this book
should serve only as a general guide and not as the
ultimate source of subject information.
This book contains information that might be dated and
is intended only to educate and entertain.
The author and publisher shall have no liability or
responsibility to any person or entity regarding any loss or
damage incurred, or alleged to have incurred, directly
or indirectly, by the information contained in this book.

CONTENTS

CONTENTS

CONTENTS

INTRODUCTION

There often comes a point when we wish there was a real life equivalent of the CTRL+ALT+DEL button. Just three strokes on the computer keyboard that can undo whatever has gone wrong and reset to 'factory settings'.

When it comes to our health and weight unfortunately there is no such 'quick fix' despite the claims of many 'fad' diets' that promise the earth. Dropping pounds rapidly is seen as the holy grail but ultimately quick fix weight loss plans are mostly unsustainable and often result in 'yo-yo' dieting where weight piles back on soon after finishing the diet.

The levels of adult (and child) obesity in North America and in the western world are now at critical levels. 1 in 3 adults are also considered to be overweight. According to the National Center for Health Statistics, nearly 40% of American adults and 19% of young people are obese with middle-aged people the most likely age group to fall into that category.

With such epidemic health issues and the host of associated conditions that so often come with being overweight such as type 2 diabetes, heart disease, stroke, kidney disease and high blood pressure, there is an urgent need for action.

Contrastingly while the US population continues to pile on the pounds, the popularity of the fitness industry is soaring. So why is it that weight and obesity problems don't appear to be effectively tackled by the fitness industry? There are many factors that contribute to the answer including our attitude to food and more importantly nutrition as well as the unrealistic image of health and body composition that the fitness industry so often uses to sell it's products. Also a key factor is human nature and the need for that 'quick fix'. When we are faced with a problem and we put our minds to tackle it, we instinctively want a solution...and fast. It's natural to want the problem to be solved as quickly as possible so we can get on with our lives. So when we see claims of rapid weight loss in the shortest possible time, we're hooked. Who wouldn't want to shed those extra pounds in a matter of days and look and feel great?

The problem is you can feel awful while you jump on the magical weight loss bandwagon literally starving your body of its essential nutrients and, whilst you may lose weight rapidly, what happens after this detox period? How do you sustain the weight loss or maintain your new 'happy' weight? The answer more often than not is ....you don't.

Your body is craving the macro-nutrients (protein, carbs and good fats) it has been starved of and this craving results in poor food choices that take you back to square one or sometimes cause weight gain.
Also your body is clever; because it has literally been starved, when you do start eating normally again it is more likely to store energy as fat in preparation for the next period of starvation that you unleash upon your body ...and so the cycle continues.

Step up to the mic....

Harley Pasternak is a celebrity fitness trainer, holds a master's degree in exercise physiology and nutritional sciences from the University of Toronto, co-hosted ABC's "The Revolution" talk show and is the creator of The Body Reset Diet. He has worked with celebrities such as Alicia Keys, Rihanna, Lady Gaga, Kanye West, Bono and Megan Fox

In his best-selling book The Body Reset Diet: Power Your Metabolism, Blast Fat, and Shed Pounds In Just 15 Days he recognizes the desire in human nature to see results quickly. He has devised a solution to lose weight rapidly while continuing to feed the body with essential and balanced macro-nutrients on a daily basis, primarily though the consumption of delicious plant-based smoothies over a period of 15 days. The Body Reset Diet cranks up the metabolism, kicking it into gear by encouraging eating 5 times a day over 3 phases slowly reintroducing solid food back into the diet. His combination of reduced calorie smoothie 'meals' coupled with daily exercise of (easily obtainable) 10,000 steps and basic resistance training helps train your body to use energy more efficiently and burn calories faster, resetting the body and guiding it onto a new and better path of sustainable, nutritionally sound eating and exercise for the rest of your life.

In the *Body Reset Diet Plan*, **phase 1** consists of mainly drinking smoothies for your meals with two 'crunchy' snacks. The smoothies are grouped by color –white smoothies (contain milk or Greek yogurt, a good source of protein), red (full of fruit for energy & fiber) and green (comprised of vegetables for additional fiber and to keep you full).

In **phase 2** you drink two smoothies per day, replacing one meal with solid food.

Phase 3 replaces one more smoothie for another solid meal.

Pasternak sees the initial weight loss results as a real motivator. When achieved quickly they will spur us on to think more carefully about what we eat and when we eat to maintain a happy, healthier weight long term.

The satisfaction of seeing weight drop off quickly without depriving yourself is the key motivating factor in sticking with the plan.

We recommend you study Pasternak's book The Body Reset Diet for a full understanding of the 3-phase plan including recipes for snacks and meals in phases 2 and 3.

The content of our book focuses purely on a collection of delicious calorie counted smoothies to use as part of your Body Reset Plan. Our simple, balanced smoothie recipes can be incorporated into your plan and bring variety to make sure you stay motivated.

Our recipes are divided into three sections – breakfast (mostly 'white' smoothies), lunch (mostly 'red' smoothies) and dinner (mostly 'green' smoothies). It is not necessary to follow this plan exactly. For example you can choose a green smoothie for breakfast and a red smoothie for dinner if you prefer as long as you have one smoothie from each group per day (in phase 1) in line with the Body Reset Diet plan. Each smoothie includes protein, healthy fats and carbohydrates.

Please note that Pasternak advises that if you are over 174llbs/79kg/12.5 stone then you should increase serving sizes by one third to ensure you get all the nutrition and energy needed.

All the recipes in this book have been tested using the Nutribullet 600 series blender (large cup) but they can be adjusted for use with any quality personal blender on the market.

Blending Tips

Personal blenders are simple and easy to use. Follow these tips to get the most from your device:

• When using ice in your drink, always immerse the ice first in a little liquid. You can do this in the sports bottle with the liquid ingredients you are using such as a little water or fruit juice.

• When you are adding ingredients don't fill the sports bottle above the max line.

• If some ingredients become stuck around the blade just detach the bottle from the base unit and give it a good shake to loosen the ingredients then blend again.

• Clean the blender base unit with a damp cloth. The blade, bottle and cap can all be placed in a dishwasher or alternatively wash with warm soapy water. For best results wash parts immediately after using.

• For stubborn ingredients that may have stuck to the blade or the inside of the bottle, half fill the bottle with warm water and a drop or two of detergent, fit the blade and attach to the base unit pulsing for 10 seconds or so.

• Use the freshest produce available. We recommend buying organic produce whenever you can if your budget allows. You can also freeze your fruit to preserve it.

• Wash your fruit and veg before blending to remove any traces of bacteria, pesticides and insects.

- The type of blender you have will dictate which seeds and skins should be removed from fruit and vegetables. However the following seeds and pits should always be removed before blending as they may contain chemicals which can release cyanide into the body when ingested so do not use any of the following in your smoothies:

  - » *Apple Seeds*
  - » *Cherry Pits*
  - » *Peach pits*
  - » *Apricot Pits*
  - » *Plum Pits*

- Chop ingredients, especially harder produce, into small pieces to ensure smoother blending.

All Recipes Are A Guide Only

All the recipes in this book are a guide only. You may need to alter quantities to suit your own appliances.

About CookNation

CookNation is the leading publisher of innovative and practical recipe books for the modern, health conscious cook.

CookNation titles bring together delicious, easy and practical recipes with their unique approach - easy and delicious, no-nonsense recipes - making cooking for diets and healthy eating fast, simple and fun.

With a range of #1 best-selling titles - from the innovative 'Skinny' calorie-counted series, to the 5:2 Diet Recipes collection - CookNation recipe books prove that 'Diet' can still mean 'Delicious'!

 **CookNation**

THE
BODY
RESET
DIET

BREAKFAST
SMOOTHIES

ALMOND & ORANGE SMOOTHIE

380 calories

Ingredients

- 1 shredded romaine lettuce
- 2 oranges
- 125g/4oz carrot
- 1 tbsp chopped fresh mint

- 1 tbsp almonds
- 250ml/1 cup unsweetened almond milk
- 2 tbsp non fat Greek yogurt
- Water

Method

1 Rinse the ingredients well.

2 Peel the oranges and separate into segments, don't worry about the pips.

3 Scrub the carrots, removing and discarding the tops before chopping.

4 Add all the fruit, vegetables, almonds, youghurt & milk to the blender. Make sure the ingredients do not go past the MAX line on your machine.

5 Add water, again being careful not to exceed the MAX line.

6 Blend until smooth.

CHEF'S NOTE
Optional protein boost: Add 1 tablespoon of protein powder.

SWEET PINEAPPLE JUICE

390 calories

Ingredients

- 50g/2oz spinach
- 1 banana
- 200g/7oz fresh peeled pineapple

- 250ml/1 cup soya milk
- 2 tsp chia seeds
- 2 tbsp non fat Greek yogurt

Method

1 Rinse the ingredients well.

2 Peel the banana and break into three pieces.

3 Add the fruit, vegetables, seeds, soya milk & Greek yogurt to the blender making sure the ingredients do not go past the MAX line on your machine.

4 Blend until smooth.

CHEF'S NOTE
Add water if you wish to make this a longer drink.

CASHEW CLEANSE

415 calories

Ingredients

GOOD FATS ➡️

- 50g/2oz spinach
- 1 banana
- 75g/3oz fresh peeled pineapple
- 250ml/1 cup unsweetened almond milk
- 10 fresh cashew nuts
- 75g/3oz silken tofu
- Water

Method

1 Rinse the ingredients well.

2 Peel the banana and break each into three pieces.

3 Add all the fruit, vegetables, nuts, tofu & milk to the blender. Make sure the ingredients do not go past the MAX line on your machine.

4 Add water, again being careful not to exceed the MAX line.

5 Blend until smooth.

CHEF'S NOTE
Optional boost: Add 1 teaspoon of flax or chia seeds.

LIME & CRANBERRY SMOOTHIE

375 calories

Ingredients

- 250ml/1 cup soya milk
- 1 apple
- 2-3 tbsp lime juice
- 75g/3oz silken tofu

- 1 banana
- 200g/7oz fresh cranberries
- 1 tbsp pumpkin seeds
- Water

Method

1 Rinse the ingredients well.

2 Core the apple, leaving the skin on (if you have a high powered blender)..

3 Add all the fruit, vegetables, milk, tofu & seeds to the blender. Make sure the ingredients do not go past the MAX line on your machine.

4 Add water, again being careful not to exceed the MAX line.

5 Blend until smooth.

CHEF'S NOTE
Adjust the quantity of lime to suit your taste.

SALAD & BANANA BLASTER

340 calories

Ingredients

- 1 shredded romaine lettuce
- 1 pear
- 1 banana
- 250ml/1 cup 1% milk

- 2 tbsp non fat Greek yogurt
- 1 tbsp ground almonds
- Water

Method

1 Rinse the ingredients well.

2 Core the pear, leaving the skin on. Peel the banana and break into three pieces.

3 Add all the fruit, lettuce, yogurt, almonds and milk to the blender. Make sure the ingredients do not go past the MAX line on your machine.

4 Add water, again being careful not to exceed the MAX line.

5 Blend until smooth.

CHEF'S NOTE
Optional boost: Add 1 tablespoon of acai berries.

LEMON & GINGER SOYA SMOOTHIE

480 calories

Ingredients

- 50g/2oz spinach
- 3 tbsp lemon juice
- 1 banana
- 150g/5oz fresh peeled pineapple
- ½ small avocado

- 2cm/1 inch fresh ginger root
- 250ml/1 cup soya milk
- 2 tbsp non fat Greek yogurt
- Water

Method

1 Rinse the ingredients well.

2 Peel the banana and break into three pieces.

3 De-stone and peel the avocado.

4 Add all the fruit, vegetables, yogurt and milk to the blender. Make sure the ingredients do not go past the MAX line on your machine.

5 Add water, again being careful not to exceed the MAX line.

6 Blend until smooth.

CHEF'S NOTE
Avocado is a great source of healthy fats

CARROT & RAISIN NUT SMOOTHIE

420 calories

Ingredients

HIGH ENERGY →

- ½ avocado
- 50g/2oz carrot
- 1 tbsp ground almonds
- 125g/4oz spinach
- 250ml/1 cup unsweetened almond milk
- ½ tsp cinnamon
- 2 tbsp non fat Greek yogurt

Method

1 Wash the carrot and spinach. Nip the ends off the carrot.

2 Peel and de-stone the avocado.

3 Add everything to the blender. Make sure the ingredients do not go past the MAX line on your machine.

4 Top up with water if needed to take it up to the MAX line.

5 Blend until smooth.

CHEF'S NOTE
Almond milk is low in fat and high in energy, proteins, lipids and fibre.

BANANA SOYA MILK

390 calories

Ingredients

- 2 bananas
- 3 tbsp non fat Greek yogurt
- 120ml/½ cup soya milk
- 1 tsp honey

- Pinch of ground cinnamon
- 1 tbsp finely chopped walnuts
- Ice

Method

1 Peel the bananas and break each into three pieces.

2 Add everything to the blender, finishing with ice. Make sure you don't go past the MAX line on your machine.

3 Blend until smooth.

CHEF'S NOTE
Experiment with more cinnamon for a warmer, spicier taste.

CHERRY GREEN SMOOTHIE

395 calories

Ingredients

- 50g/2oz spinach
- 150g/5oz pitted cherries
- 1 banana
- 250ml/1 cup unsweetened almond milk
- 1 tbsp coconut oil
- 1 tsp ground almonds
- Water

Method

1 Rinse the ingredients well.

2 Remove any thick stalks from the spinach.

3 Peel the banana. Make sure you have removed all the stalks and stones from the cherries.

4 Add the spinach, fruit, oil, almonds & almond milk to the blender. Make sure the ingredients do not go past the MAX line on your machine.

5 Add a little water if needed to take it up to the MAX line.

6 Blend until smooth.

CHEF'S NOTE
Pitted frozen cherries are a great shortcut ingredient for making this smoothie.

PINEAPPLE PROTEIN SHAKE

450 calories

Ingredients

- 1 banana
- 200g/7oz fresh peeled pineapple
- 1 tbsp almonds
- 1 scoop protein powder
- 120ml/½ cup soya milk
- Water

Method

1 Rinse the ingredients well.

2 Peel the banana and break into three pieces.

3 Add the fruit, almonds, milk & protein powder to the blender. Make sure the ingredients do not go past the MAX line on your machine.

4 Add water, again being careful not to exceed the MAX line.

5 Blend until smooth.

CHEF'S NOTE
Optional boost: Add 1 tablespoon of goji berries.

FRESH ALMOND & PEAR SMOOTHIE

365 calories

Ingredients

- 1 pear
- 1 banana
- 250ml/1 cup unsweetened almond milk
- 1 tbsp ground almonds
- 3 tbsp non fat Greek yogurt
- Water

Method

1 Rinse the ingredients well.

2 Core the pear, leaving the skin on. Peel the banana and break into three pieces.

3 Add the fruit, milk, yogurt & almonds to the blender. Make sure the ingredients do not go past the MAX line on your machine.

4 Add water, again being careful not to exceed the MAX line.

5 Blend until smooth.

CHEF'S NOTE
Optional healthy fats boost: Add 1 teaspoon of hemp seeds.

OAT & CHIA SEED MORNING BLASTER

395 calories

Ingredients

- 1 banana
- 1 tsp chia seeds
- 2 tbsp rolled oats
- 1 scoop protein powder

- 250ml/1 cup soya milk
- 1 tsp honey
- Water

Method

1 Rinse the ingredients well.

2 Peel the banana and break into three pieces.

3 Add the banana, chia seeds, oats, protein powder & milk to the blender. Make sure the ingredients do not go past the MAX line on your machine.

4 Add water, again being careful not to exceed the MAX line.

5 Blend until smooth.

CHEF'S NOTE
Try a handful of blueberries if you want to add some extra sweetness.

VANILLA & OAT SMOOTHIE

410 calories

Ingredients

- 125g/4oz spinach
- 1 tsp vanilla extract
- 250ml/1 cup oat milk
- 1 tbsp cashew nuts
- 5 pitted dates
- Water
- Ice cubes

Method

1 Rinse the spinach well and place in the blender.

2 Add the oat milk, vanilla, dates, nuts and a few ice cubes. Make sure the ingredients do not go past the MAX line on your machine.

3 Add water if needed to take it up to the MAX line.

4 Blend until smooth.

CHEF'S NOTE
Use dried sweet pitted dates.

ALMOND BUTTER SPINACH SMOOTHIE

420 calories

Ingredients

- ½ ripe avocado
- 1 tbsp almond butter
- 2 tsp flax seeds
- 3 tbsp non fat Greek yogurt

- 125g/4oz spinach
- 250ml/1 cup unsweetened almond milk
- Ice cubes

Method

1 Rinse the spinach and roughly chop. Peel and de-stone the avocado.

2 Add all the ingredients to the blender. Make sure they do not go past the MAX line on your machine.

3 Blend until smooth.

CHEF'S NOTE
Almond butter is good source of vitamin E, copper & magnesium.

MILK MINT SMOOTHIE

365 calories

Ingredients

- 1 apple
- 1 tbsp lemon juice
- 1 scoop protein powder
- ¼ cucumber

- 1 tbsp chopped fresh mint
- 250ml/1 cup soya milk
- 1 tbsp chopped pistachios
- Water

Method

1 Rinse the ingredients well.

2 Core the apple, leaving the skin on.

3 Dice the cucumber, leaving the skin on.

4 Add all the ingredients to the blender. Making sure they do not go past the MAX line on your machine.

5 Blend until smooth.

CHEF'S NOTE
Adjust the quantity of mint to suit your taste.

MORNING GLORY AVOCADO SMOOTHIE

389
calories

Ingredients

- 50g/2oz spinach
- ½ ripe avocado
- 1 apple
- 250ml/1 cup 1% milk

- 1 banana
- 2 tsp pumpkin seeds
- Water

Method

1 Rinse the ingredients well.

2 Scoop out the avocado flesh discarding the rind & stone.

3 Core the apple, leaving the skin on. Peel the banana and break into three pieces.

4 Add the fruit, vegetables & seeds to the blender. Make sure the ingredients do not go past the MAX line on your machine.

5 Add water, again being careful not to exceed the MAX line.

6 Blend until smooth.

CHEF'S NOTE
Try flax seeds as an alternative to pumpkin seeds.

MELON & CASHEW GREEN SMOOTHIE

360 calories

Ingredients

- 50g/2oz spinach
- 1 apple
- 200g/7oz cantaloupe melon
- 250ml/1 cup 1% milk

- 1 tbsp cashew nuts
- 75g/3oz silken tofu
- Water

Method

1 Rinse the ingredients well.

2 Core the apple, leaving the skin on.

3 Scoop out the melon flesh, discarding the seeds & rind.

4 Add the fruit, vegetables, tofu & nuts to the blender. Make sure the ingredients do not go past the MAX line on your machine.

5 Add water, again being careful not to exceed the MAX line.

6 Blend until smooth.

CHEF'S NOTE
Try almonds or walnuts in place of the cashew nuts.

HONEY WALNUT SMOOTHIE

420 calories

Ingredients

- 1 orange
- 200g/7oz mixed berries
- 250ml/1 cup unsweetened almond milk
- 1 tsp honey

- 8 walnuts halves
- 1 scoop protein powder
- Water

Method

1 Rinse the ingredients well.

2 Peel the orange and separate into segments.

3 Add the fruit, milk, honey, protein powder & walnuts to the blender. Make sure the ingredients do not go past the MAX line on your machine.

4 Add water, again being careful not to exceed the MAX line.

5 Blend until smooth.

CHEF'S NOTE
The fresh walnuts should be shelled before adding to the cup.

BRIGHT GINGER SMOOTHIE

385 calories

Ingredients

- 1 apple
- 4cm/2 inch fresh peeled ginger
- 1 tbsp honey
- 2 tbsp non fat Greek yogurt

- 1 banana
- 1 tbsp lemon juice
- 250ml/1 cup unsweetened almond milk
- 6 walnut halves

Method

1 Finely grate the ginger.

2 Core the apple. Chop the walnuts.

3 Peel the banana and break into three pieces.

4 Add everything to the blender. Make sure the ingredients do not go past the MAX line on your machine.

5 Add a little water if needed to take it up to the MAX line.

6 Blend until smooth.

CHEF'S NOTE

Ginger is prized for it's healing and detoxifying properties.

GREEN SOYA PUMPKIN MILK

435 calories

Ingredients

- 1 pear
- 1 apple
- 50g/2oz spinach
- 250ml/1 cup soya milk

- 2 tbsp non fat Greek yogurt
- 1 tbsp pumpkin seeds
- Water

Method

1 Wash the spinach and the pear. Core the pear and apple but don't peel them.

2 Add all the ingredients except water to the blender. Make sure they do not go past the MAX line on your machine.

3 Add a little water if needed to take it up to the MAX line.

4 Blend until smooth.

CHEF'S NOTE
Pumpkin seeds provide heart-healthy magnesium.

MINT & CHIA GREEN SMOOTHIE

310 calories

Ingredients

- 75g/3oz spinach
- 1 banana
- ¼ ripe avocado
- 1 tbsp chopped fresh mint

- 2 tsp chia seeds
- 250ml/1 cup unsweetened almond milk
- Water

Method

1 Rinse the spinach. Peel the banana. Peel and de-stone the avocado.

2 Add everything to the blender. Make sure the ingredients do not go past the MAX line on your machine.

3 Add a little water if needed to take it up to the MAX line.

4 Blend until smooth.

CHEF'S NOTE
Chia seeds can help raise HDL cholesterol – which is the good cholesterol that helps protect against heart attack and stroke.

DATE & BANANA SMOOTHIE

390 calories

Ingredients

- 1 banana
- 4 pitted dates
- ¼ ripe avocado

- 250ml/1 cup unsweetened almond milk
- Large pinch ground cinnamon
- 1 scoop protein powder

Method

1 Peel the banana. Halve the dates.

2 Peel and stone the avocado.

3 Add everything to the blender. Make sure the ingredients do not go past the MAX line on your machine.

4 Blend until smooth.

CHEF'S NOTE

Feel free to add more almond milk as far as the MAX line if you wish, but remember it will increase your calorie intake.

SUPER SWEET SMOOTHIE

325 calories

Ingredients

- 2 tsp honey
- 75g/3oz spinach
- 200g/7oz pineapple
- 1 apple
- 250ml/1 cup unsweetened almond milk
- 1 tsp ground almonds
- Water

Method

1 Rinse the ingredients well.

2 Cut any thick stalks off the spinach.

3 Peel the pineapple. Core the apple.

4 Add the spinach, fruit & honey to the blender. Make sure the ingredients do not go past the MAX line on your machine.

5 Add water, again being careful not to exceed the MAX line.

6 Blend until smooth.

CHEF'S NOTE
High in fibre and with zero fat, spinach is a mega-smoothie super-food.

TOTALLY TROPICAL

350 calories

Ingredients

- 150g/5oz mango
- 150g/5oz pineapple
- 1 banana
- 1 tbsp cashew nuts

- 2 tbsp Greek yogurt
- 250ml/1 cup soya milk
- Ice

Method

1 Peel the pineapple and banana.

2 Peel & de-stone the mango.

3 Add the fruit to the blender. Make sure the ingredients do not go past the MAX line on your machine.

4 Add ice, again being careful not to exceed the MAX line.

5 Blend until smooth.

CHEF'S NOTE
You could try making with oat milk too.

VIT C + SMOOTHIE MILK

385 calories

Ingredients

- 2 passion fruits
- ½ banana
- 120ml/½ cup soya milk
- 2 tsp hemp seeds

- 50g/2oz pineapple
- 2 tbsp non fat Greek yogurt
- Water

Method

1 Scoop out the flesh of the passion fruits, discarding the skins.

2 Peel the banana and the pineapple.

3 Add everything to the blender, making sure the ingredients do not go past the MAX line on your machine.

4 Add a little water if needed to take it up to the MAX line.

5 Blend until smooth.

CHEF'S NOTE

For extra creaminess, use a whole banana.

WATERMELON & CHIA SEED SMOOTHIE

350 calories

Ingredients

- 250g/9oz watermelon
- 1 tbsp chia seeds
- 1 apple
- 250ml/1 cup unsweetened almond milk
- 1 tsp honey
- 1 scoop protein powder
- Water
- Ice

Method

1 Scoop out the watermelon flesh, de-seed and place in the blender.

2 Core the apple.

3 Add all the other ingredients, finishing with ice as far as the MAX line on your machine.

4 Blend until smooth.

CHEF'S NOTE

Watermelon is believed to have the most potent cancer-fighting properties of any fruit.

MANGO YOGURT SMOOTHIE

310 calories

Ingredients

- 125g/4oz mango
- 4 tbsp natural low-fat Greek yogurt
- 250ml/1 cup unsweetened almond milk
- 1 tsp honey
- 2 tsp ground almonds
- Water

Method

1 Peel and de-stone the mango.

2 Add to the blender, along with the other ingredients.

3 Make sure the ingredients do not go past the MAX line on your machine.

4 Add a little water if needed to take it up to the MAX line.

5 Blend until smooth.

CHEF'S NOTE
Make sure your mango is ripe for maximum sweetness!

LUNCH
SMOOTHIES

SWEET SOYA SMOOTHIE

325 calories

Ingredients

FRUITY GOODNESS →

- 50g/2oz spinach
- 150g/5oz strawberries
- 250ml/1 cup soya milk
- 1 tsp runny honey
- 1 tsp hemp seeds
- Water

Method

1 Rinse the ingredients well.

2 Add all the ingredients to the blender. Make sure the ingredients do not go past the MAX line on your machine.

3 Add water (if there's space), again being careful not to exceed the MAX line.

4 Blend until smooth.

CHEF'S NOTE
Optional boost: Add 1 tablespoon of shelled fresh walnuts.

FLAX SEED & BERRY BLAST

390 calories

Ingredients

- 50g/2oz spinach
- 1 banana
- 250g/9oz raspberries
- 1 scoop protein powder
- 1 tbsp flax seeds
- 250ml/1 cup unsweetened almond milk
- Water

Method

1 Rinse the ingredients well.

2 Peel the banana and break into three pieces.

3 Add all the ingredients to the blender. Make sure the ingredients do not go past the MAX line on your machine.

4 Add water, again being careful not to exceed the MAX line.

5 Blend until smooth.

CHEF'S NOTE
Any berries work well in this power packed smoothie.

FRUITY FLAX SEED SMOOTHIE

SERVES 1

360 calories

Ingredients

VITAMIN C +

- 50g/2oz spinach
- 75g/3oz mixed berries
- 175g/6oz fresh mango
- 1 banana
- 3 tbsp non fat Greek yogurt
- 2 tsp of flax seeds
- Water

Method

1 Rinse the ingredients well.

2 De-stone and peel the mango. Peel the banana and break into three pieces.

3 Add all the ingredients to the blender. Make sure the ingredients do not go past the MAX line on your machine.

4 Add water, again being careful not to exceed the MAX line.

5 Blend until smooth.

CHEF'S NOTE
Try with coconut water too.

PEAR & ALMOND YOGURT SMOOTHIE

335 calories

Ingredients

- 1 tbsp almonds
- 100g/3½oz apple
- 1 banana
- 2 tbsp low fat Greek yogurt

- 250ml/1 cup unsweetened almond milk
- ½ tsp ground cinnamon
- Water

Method

1 Rinse and core the apple.

2 Peel the banana and break into three pieces.

3 Add all the ingredients to the blender. Make sure they do not go past the MAX line on your machine.

4 Add a little water if needed to take it up to the MAX line.

5 Blend until smooth.

CHEF'S NOTE
Almonds contain useful antioxidants which cleanse toxins.

BLUEBERRY OAT MILK

310 calories

Ingredients

FILLING SMOOTHIE ➤

- 100g/3½oz blueberries
- 180ml/¾ cup light oat milk
- A pinch of ground cinnamon
- 1 tsp honey
- 1 tbsp chia seeds
- Water

Method

1 Rinse the blueberries. Add them to the blender, along with the other ingredients, making sure not go past the MAX line on your machine.

2 Add a little water if needed to take it up to the MAX line.

3 Blend until smooth.

CHEF'S NOTE
Chia seeds contain high amounts of both soluble and insoluble fibre, and help to clean out the digestive tract.

AVOCADO CACAO SMOOTHIE

400 calories

Ingredients

- 250ml/1 cup 1% milk
- ½o avocado
- 75g/3oz raspberries
- 1 tbsp cacao powder
- 75g/3oz spinach
- 1 tbsp pecan nuts

Method

1 Rinse the raspberries and spinach well.

2 Peel and de-stone the avocado.

3 Add all the ingredients to the blender. Make sure they don't go past the MAX line on your machine.

4 Blend until smooth.

CHEF'S NOTE

Raw cacao contains nearly four times the antioxidant content of processed dark chocolate.

GRAPEFRUIT SWEET JUICE

335 calories

Ingredients

- 250ml/1 cup grapefruit juice
- 1 apple
- 200g/7oz mixed berries
- 1 tsp hemp seeds
- 1 tsp honey
- 2 tbsp non fat Greek yogurt
- Water

Method

1 Rinse the ingredients well.

2 Core the apple.

3 Add all the ingredients to the blender. Make sure the ingredients do not go past the MAX line on your machine.

4 Add water, again being careful not to exceed the MAX line.

5 Blend until smooth.

CHEF'S NOTE

Optional boost: Add 1 teaspoon of sunflower seeds.

BERRY CASHEW SMOOTHIE

440
calories

Ingredients

- 50g/2oz spinach
- 1 banana
- 125g/3oz strawberries
- 1 scoop protein powder

- 10 cashew nuts
- 250ml/1 cup unsweetened almond milk
- Water

Method

1 Rinse the ingredients well.

2 Peel the banana and break into three pieces.

3 Add all the ingredients to the blender. Make sure the ingredients do not go past the MAX line on your machine.

4 Add water, again being careful not to exceed the MAX line.

5 Blend until smooth.

CHEF'S NOTE
Cashew nuts are packed with vitamins, minerals and antioxidants.

CARROT CLEANSER

315 calories

Ingredients

- 1 handful shredded lettuce
- 250ml/1 cup unsweetened soya milk
- 1 apple
- 1 banana
- 150g/5oz carrots
- 1 tsp honey
- 1 tsp cashew nuts
- Water

Method

1 Rinse the ingredients well.

2 Core the apple, leaving the skin on. Peel the banana and break into three pieces.

3 Nip the ends off the carrots and chop.

4 Add all the ingredients to the blender. Make sure the ingredients do not go past the MAX line on your machine.

5 Add water, again being careful not to exceed the MAX line.

6 Blend until smooth.

CHEF'S NOTE

Adjust the honey to suit your own taste.

SPRING GOJI BERRY SMOOTHIE

325 calories

Ingredients

- 50g/2oz shredded spring greens
- 150g/5oz strawberries
- 1 banana
- 2 tbsp goji berries
- 250ml/1 cup unsweetened almond milk
- 2 tbsp non fat Greek yogurt
- Water

Method

1 Rinse the ingredients well.

2 Cut the green tops off the strawberries.

3 Peel the banana and break into three pieces.

4 Add all the ingredients to the blender. Make sure the ingredients do not go past the MAX line on your machine.

5 Add water (if there's space), again being careful not to exceed the MAX line.

6 Blend until smooth.

CHEF'S NOTE
Use spinach if you can't get spring greens.

CHIA & SOYA PINEAPPLE SMOOTHIE

375 calories

Ingredients

- 50g/2oz spinach
- 1 banana
- 100g/3½oz fresh peeled pineapple
- 3 tbsp non fat Greek yogurt
- 250ml/1 cup soya milk
- 1 tsp chia seeds
- Water

Method

1 Rinse the ingredients well.

2 Peel the banana and break into three pieces.

3 Add the fruit, vegetables, seeds, milk & yogurt to your blender. Make sure the ingredients do not go past the MAX line on your machine.

4 Add water, again being careful not to exceed the MAX line.

5 Blend until smooth.

CHEF'S NOTE

You could also try this with almond milk.

WALNUT BLUEBERRY SMOOTHIE

348 calories

Ingredients

- 50g/2oz spinach
- 1 banana
- 100g/3½oz blueberries
- 1 scopp protein powder
- 250ml/1 cup unsweetened almond milk
- 6 walnut halves
- Water

Method

1 Rinse the ingredients well.

2 Peel the banana and break into three pieces.

3 Add the fruit, vegetables, milk, protein & nuts to the blender. Make sure the ingredients do not go past the MAX line on your machine.

4 Add water, again being careful not to exceed the MAX line.

5 Blend until smooth.

CHEF'S NOTE
Walnuts are a good source of vitamin E, folate, melatonin, omega-3 fats, and antioxidants.

RED COCONUT MILK SMOOTHIE

420 calories

Ingredients

- 50g/2oz strawberries
- 50g/2oz rapsberries
- 3 tbsp non fat Greek yogurt
- 1 banana

- 250ml/1 cup low fat coconut milk
- 1 tsp honey
- 1 tsp pumpkin seeds
- Water

Method

1 Rinse the ingredients well.

2 Peel the banana and break into three pieces.

3 Add the fruit, yogurt, milk, seeds & honey to the blender. Making sure they do not go past the MAX line on your machine.

4 Add water, again being careful not to exceed the MAX line.

5 Blend until smooth.

CHEF'S NOTE
Greek yogurt is a good source of lean protein

BANANA & HEMP SEED SMOOTHIE

395 calories

Ingredients

- 1 banana
- 125g/4oz mixed berries
- 250ml/1 cup soya almond milk
- 2 tsp hemp seeds
- 1 scoop protein powder
- Water

Method

1 Peel the banana.

2 Rinse the berries and nip off any green tops.

3 Place the ingredients in the blender making sure the ingredients do not go past the MAX line on your machine.

4 Top up with a little water if you like & blend until smooth.

CHEF'S NOTE
Hemp seed is rich in omega 3 and omega 6.

GINGER BEETROOT FRUIT JUICE

355 calories

Ingredients

- 50g/2oz spinach
- 1 fresh medium beetroot
- 1 pear
- 1 apple

- 250ml/1 cup 1% milk
- 50g/2oz silken tofu
- 2cm/1 inch fresh ginger root
- Water

Method

1 Rinse the ingredients well.

2 Remove any thick stalks from the spinach.

3 Cut the green stalks off the beetroot and dice.

4 Core the apple & pear, leave the skin on.

5 Add all the ingredients to the blender. Make sure the ingredients do not go past the MAX line on your machine.

6 Add water, again being careful not to exceed the MAX line.

7 Blend until smooth.

CHEF'S NOTE
Optional boost: Add 1 teaspoon flax seeds.

FRUITY OAT SMOOTHIE

380 calories

Ingredients

- 125g/4oz strawberries
- 1 banana
- 250ml/1 cup unsweetened almond milk
- 2 slices avocado

- 2 tbsp rolled oats
- 1 scoop protein powder
- Water

Method

1 Rinse the strawberries well and nip off the green tops.

2 Peel the banana.

3 Add all the ingredients to the blender. Make sure the ingredients do not go past the MAX line on your machine.

4 Add a little more water if needed to take it up to the MAX line.

5 Blend until smooth.

CHEF'S NOTE
Strawberries are great for cleansing due to the antioxidants and fibre.

CHOCOLATE RASPBERRY SOYA MILK

390 calories

Ingredients

- 1 banana
- 1 tbsp dark cocoa powder
- 250ml/1 cup soya milk
- 125g/4oz raspberries
- 3 tbsp non fat Greek yogurt
- 2 tsp ground almonds
- Ice

Method

1 Peel the banana.

2 Rinse the strawberries and remove the green tops.

3 Place them in the blender together with all the other ingredients, Make sure it doesn't go past the MAX line on your machine.

4 Blend until smooth.

CHEF'S NOTE
Dark cocoa contains antioxidants that regular cocoa doesn't have.

ALMOND & MANGO SMOOTHIE

420 calories

Ingredients

- 200g/7oz mango
- 1 banana
- 250ml/1 cup unsweetened almond milk
- 1 tbsp almonds
- 2 tbsp non fat Greek yogurt
- Water

Method

1 Peel, stone and cube the mango.

2 Peel the banana.

3 Add everything to the blender. Make sure the ingredients do not go past the MAX line on your machine.

4 Blend until smooth.

CHEF'S NOTE

Bananas are rich in fibre, vitamins B6, and minerals like potassium and manganese, which make them very nutritious and great for detox.

DOUBLE BERRY JUICE

385 calories

Ingredients

- 50g/2oz spinach
- 1 banana
- 125g/4oz mixed berries
- 6 walnut halves

- 1 scoop protein powder
- Small pinch ground cinnamon
- 3 tbsp non fat Greek yogurt
- Water

Method

1 Rinse the ingredients well.

2 Remove any thick stalks from the spinach.

3 Peel the banana and break into three pieces.

4 Add all the ingredients to the blender. Make sure the ingredients do not go past the MAX line on your machine.

5 Add water, again being careful not to exceed the MAX line.

6 Blend until smooth.

CHEF'S NOTE
Feel free to experiment with the cinnamon quantity in this recipe - you may prefer a little more.

NUTMEG PINEAPPLE CLEANSE

375 calories

Ingredients

- 1 banana
- 2 tbsp goji berries
- 120ml/½ oat milk
- 125g/4oz pineapple
- 2 tbsp non fat Greek yogurt
- ¼ tsp ground nutmeg
- Water

Method

1 Peel the banana and pineapple.

2 Add everything to the blender. Make sure the ingredients do not go past the MAX line on your machine.

3 Add a little water if needed to take it up to the MAX line.

4 Blend until smooth.

CHEF'S NOTE
Nutmeg increases immune system function.

GOJI BERRY COCONUT BLASTER

410
calories

Ingredients

- 250ml/1 cup coconut water
- 1 tbsp coconut cream
- ½ ripe avocado
- 3 tbsp non fat Greek yogurt
- 100g/3½oz strawberries
- 1 tbsp goji berries
- Water

Method

1 Rinse the strawberries and remove the green tops.

2 Peel & de-stone the avocado.

3 Add all the ingredients to the blender. Make sure they don't go past the MAX line on your machine.

4 Blend until smooth.

CHEF'S NOTE
Soak goji berries in warm water for a few minutes before using.

CASHEW & SOYA MILK SMOOTHIE

300 calories

Ingredients

GOOD FATS →

- 10 cashew nuts
- 75g/3oz spinach
- 250ml/1 cup soya milk
- 125g/4oz raspberries
- 2 tbsp non fat Greek yogurt
- Ice cubes

Method

1 Rinse the spinach well.

2 Add all the ingredients to the blender, finishing with ice.

3 Make sure the ingredients do not go past the MAX line on your machine.

4 Blend until smooth.

CHEF'S NOTE
Vary the quantity of nuts to suit your own taste but be aware of the calorie count if you do this.

GINGER SPICED ORANGE JUICE

255 calories

Ingredients

- 250ml/1 cup freshly squeezed orange juice
- 1 apple
- 2 tsp grated fresh ginger
- 50g/2oz spinach
- 1 scoop protein powder
- 1 tbsp hemp seeds
- Ice cubes

Method

1 Rinse the apple and the spinach. Core and chop the apple.

2 Add all the ingredients to the blender, finishing with ice cubes to taste.

3 Make sure the ingredients do not go past the MAX line on your machine.

4 Blend until smooth.

CHEF'S NOTE
High in antioxidants, nutrients and vitamin C, fresh orange juice is a great detox ingredient.

RASPBERRY FLAX SMOOTHIE

295 calories

Ingredients

- 125g/4oz raspberries
- 1 tbsp flax seeds
- 50g/2oz spinach

- 2 tbsp non fat Greek yogurt
- 250ml/1 cup 1% milk
- Water

Method

1 Wash the spinach and raspberries well and place them in the blender.

2 Add the flax seeds, yogurt and milk. Make sure they don't go past the MAX line on your machine.

3 Top up with water as far as the MAX line.

4 Blend until smooth.

CHEF'S NOTE
Flax seeds are rich in protein and fibre.

APPLE & YOGURT SMOOTHIE

375 calories

Ingredients

- 1 apple
- 4 tbsp non fat Greek yogurt
- 1 tsp lime juice
- 1 tsp chia seeds
- ½ ripe avocado
- Water

Method

1 Rinse and core the apple.

2 Add the apple, yogurt, lime juice, avocado & chia seeds to the blender. Make sure the ingredients do not go past the MAX line on your machine.

3 Add water, again being careful not to exceed the MAX line.

4 Blend until smooth.

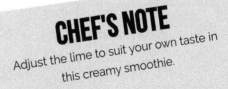

CHEF'S NOTE
Adjust the lime to suit your own taste in this creamy smoothie.

BLUEBERRY ALMOND SMOOTHIE

285 calories

Ingredients

- 25g/1oz spinach
- 150g/5oz blueberries
- 1 banana
- 1 scoop protein powder

- 250ml/1 cup unsweetened almond milk
- Water

Method

1 Rinse the ingredients well.

2 Peel the banana.

3 Add the all the ingredients to the blender. Make sure the ingredients do not go past the MAX line on your machine.

4 Add a little water if needed to take it up to the MAX line.

5 Blend until smooth.

CHEF'S NOTE
Try this recipe using cranberries instead of blueberries.

PEANUT BUTTER & ACAI SMOOTHIE

295 calories

Ingredients

- 1 banana
- 1 tbsp peanut butter
- 120ml/½ cup 1% milk
- 2 tbsp non fat Greek yogurt
- Handful of ice cubes
- 2 tbsp acai berries
- Water

Method

1 Peel the banana.

2 Add all the ingredients to the blender. Make sure the ingredients do not go past the MAX line on your machine.

3 Add water, again being careful not to exceed the MAX line.

4 Blend until smooth.

CHEF'S NOTE
Soya milk also works well in this protein rich banana smoothie.

THE
BODY
RESET
DIET

DINNER

SMOOTHIES

HONEY NUT SMOOTHIE

330
calories

Ingredients

SWEET & NUTTY ➜

- 50g/2oz spinach
- 1 apple
- 1 banana
- 1 tbsp almonds
- 1 tbsp rolled oats
- 1 tbsp runny honey
- Water

Method

1 Rinse the ingredients well.

2 Core the apple, leaving the skin on. Peel the banana and break into three pieces.

3 Add the fruit, vegetables, oats & honey to the blender. Make sure the ingredients do not go past the MAX line on your machine.

4 Add water, again being careful not to exceed the MAX line.

5 Blend until smooth.

CHEF'S NOTE
Use almond milk instead of water if you want a creamy finish.

SWEET PEPPER PICK UP JUICE

330 calories

Ingredients

- 50g/2oz spinach
- 1 yellow pepper
- 1 banana

- 200g/7oz fresh peeled pineapple
- 1 scoop protein powder
- Water

Method

1 Rinse the ingredients well.

2 Deseed the pepper, removing and discarding the stalk.

3 Peel the banana and break into three pieces.

4 Add all the ingredients to your blender.

5 Make sure the ingredients do not go past the MAX line on your machine.

6 Add water, again being careful not to exceed the MAX line.

7 Blend until smooth.

CHEF'S NOTE
Make sure you use a sweet ripe pepper for this juice.

SUPER GREEN MILK SMOOTHIE

420 calories

Ingredients

GOOD & GREEN

- 50g/2oz spinach
- 1 tbsp ground almonds
- ½ avocado
- 1 apple
- 1 pear
- 250ml/1 cup 1% milk
- Water

Method

1 Rinse the ingredients well.

2 Remove any thick stalks from the spinach.

3 Core the apple, leaving the skin on (if you have a powerful blender).

4 Add all the fruit, vegetables, nuts & milk to the blender. Make sure the ingredients do not go past the MAX line on your machine.

5 Add water, again being careful not to exceed the MAX line.

6 Blend until smooth.

CHEF'S NOTE
Try adding a twist of lemon too.

TURMERIC CLEANSER

305 calories

Ingredients

- 50g/2oz spinach
- 150g/5oz carrots
- 1 banana
- 2 tbsp non fat Greek yoghuet
- ½ tsp turmeric
- 250ml/1 cup soya milk
- 1 tbsp pumpkin seeds
- Water

Method

1 Rinse the ingredients well.

2 Scrub the carrots, discarding the tops before chopping.

3 Peel the banana and break into three pieces.

4 Add the fruit, vegetables, turmeric, seeds & milk to the blender. Make sure the ingredients do not go past the MAX line on your machine.

5 Add water, again being careful not to exceed the MAX line.

6 Blend until smooth.

CHEF'S NOTE

Turmeric is often used in traditional medicines however it can stain cooking equipment, so make sure you wash everything straight away.

PUMPKIN CARROT PROTEIN SHAKE

370 calories

Ingredients

MUSCLE BUILDER →

- 50g/2oz spinach
- 150g/5oz carrots
- 200g/7oz mixed berries
- 120ml/½ cup almond milk
- 1 tbsp pumpkin seeds
- 1 scoop protein powder
- Water

Method

1 Rinse the ingredients well.

2 Scrub and slice the carrots, discarding the tops.

3 Add the fruit, vegetables, pumpkin seeds, protein powder & almond milk to the blender. Make sure the ingredients do not go past the MAX line on your machine.

4 Add water, (if there is space) again being careful not to exceed the MAX line.

5 Blend until smooth.

CHEF'S NOTE
Optional boost: Add 1 tablespoon of goji berry seeds.

KALE & FRUIT COCONUT WATER

300 calories

Ingredients

- 50g/2oz kale
- 1 celery stalk
- 125g/4oz apple
- 3 tbsp non fat Greek yogurt
- 1 banana
- 200g/7oz fresh pineapple
- 1 tbsp pistachios
- 250ml/1 cup coconut water

Method

1 Rinse the ingredients well.

2 Remove any thick stalks from the kale.

3 Chop the celery stalk. Peel the banana and break into three pieces.

4 Core the apple, leaving the skin on.

5 Add all the ingredients to the blender. Making sure they do not go past the MAX line on your machine.

6 Blend until smooth.

CHEF'S NOTE
A spoonful of coconut cream makes a good addition.

PAPAYA & BANANA SMOOTHIE

SERVES 1

385 calories

Ingredients

- 50g/2oz spinach
- 1 banana
- 1 papaya fruit
- 1 scoop protein powder

- 150g/5oz fresh peeled pineapple
- 250ml/1 cup unsweetened almond milk
- Water

Method

1 Rinse the ingredients well.

2 Peel the banana and break into three pieces.

3 Scoop out the papaya flesh, discarding the seeds and rind.

4 Add the fruit, vegetables, protein powder & milk to the blender. Make sure the ingredients do not go past the MAX line on your machine.

5 Add water, again being careful not to exceed the MAX line.

6 Blend until smooth.

CHEF'S NOTE

Optional boost: Add 1 teaspoon of chia or flax seeds.

AVOCADO SUPER GREEN SMOOTHIE

440 calories

Ingredients

- 50g/2oz spinach
- 1 apple
- ½ ripe avocado
- 250ml/1 cup 1% milk
- 1 scoop protein powder
- Water

Method

1 Rinse the ingredients well.

2 Core the apple, leaving the skin on.

3 Scoop out the avocado flesh, discarding the stone and skin.

4 Add all the ingredients to the blender. Make sure the ingredients do not go past the MAX line on your machine.

5 Add water, again being careful not to exceed the MAX line.

6 Blend until smooth.

CHEF'S NOTE
For a dairy free version use soya milk or unsweetened almond milk.

BRIGHT BASIL BLAST

340 calories

Ingredients

- 50g/2oz spinach
- 2 apples
- 1 tbsp lime juice
- 2 tbsp non fat Greek yogurt

- 10 fresh basil leaves
- 250ml/1 cup unsweetened almond milk
- Water

Method

1 Rinse the ingredients well.

2 Core the apples, leaving the skin on.

3 Add the fruit, vegetables, lime juice, basil, yogurt & milk to the blender. Make sure the ingredients do not go past the MAX line on your machine.

4 Add water, again being careful not to exceed the MAX and blend until smooth.

CHEF'S NOTE
Optional boost: Add 1 tablespoon of fresh almonds.

GREEN GRAPE GOOD JUICE

335 calories

Ingredients

- 50g/2oz spinach
- 1 pear
- 1 apple
- 1 tbsp sunflower seeds

- 200g/7oz fresh seedless green grapes
- 250ml/1 cup soya milk
- Water

Method

1 Rinse the ingredients well.

2 Core the pear and apple, leaving the skin on.

3 Remove any stalks from the grapes.

4 Add all the fruit & vegetables to the blender. Make sure the ingredients do not go past the MAX line on your machine.

5 Add water, again being careful not to exceed the MAX line.

6 Blend until smooth.

CHEF'S NOTE
This is a really light fresh juice.

BEETROOT PROTEIN SMOOTHIE

325 calories

Ingredients

- 150g/5oz beetroot
- 1 banana
- 250ml/1 cup soya milk
- 5 pecan nuts
- 2cm/1 inch peeled fresh ginger root
- 1 scoop protein powder
- Water

Method

1 Rinse the ingredients well.

2 Peel the beetroot & banana.

3 Add the beetroot, fruit, milk, ginger, pecans & protein powder to the blender. Make sure the ingredients do not go past the MAX line on your machine.

4 Add a little water if needed to take it up to the MAX line.

5 Blend until smooth.

CHEF'S NOTE
Protein powder is a super smoothie lean protein ingredient.

GREEN GREEN SOYA MILK SMOOTHIE

360 calories

Ingredients

- 50g/2oz spinach
- 50g/2oz kale
- 1 apple
- 1 banana

- 250ml/1 cup soya milk
- 1 tbsp honey
- 2 tbsp non fat Greek yogurt
- Water

Method

1 Rinse the ingredients well.

2 Remove any thick stalks from the kale.

3 Core the apple, leaving the skin on. Peel the banana and break into three pieces.

4 Add all the fruit, vegetables, milk, yogurt & honey to the blender. Make sure the ingredients do not go past the MAX line on your machine.

5 Add water, again being careful not to exceed the MAX line.

6 Blend until smooth.

CHEF'S NOTE

Green smoothies can take a bit of getting used to but the natural sweetness of the honey, apple & banana will make them much easier to enjoy.

CREAMY AVOCADO BLEND

399 calories

Ingredients

- 1 banana
- 1 tbsp fresh flat leaf parsley
- 50g/2oz spinach
- 1 apple
- ½ ripe avocado
- 250ml/1 cup oat milk
- Ice cubes

Method

1 Rinse the parsley and spinach.

2 Peel and de-stone the avocado.

3 Core the apple and peel the banana.

4 Add all the ingredients to the blender, finishing with ice to taste, but make sure you do not go past the MAX line on your machine.

5 Blend until smooth.

CHEF'S NOTE
Parsley is rich in many vital vitamins, including Vitamin C, B 12, K and A.

SWEET KALE SMOOTHIE

305 calories

Ingredients

- 1 apple
- 1 tbsp honey
- 1 tbsp flax seeds
- 2 tbsp non fat Greek yogurt

- 50g/2oz kale
- 250ml/1 cup unsweetened almond milk
- Water

Method

1 Rinse the kale & apple.

2 Core the applem and remove the thick stalks from the kale

3 Put all the ingredients, except water, into the blender. Make sure they do not go past the MAX line on your machine.

4 Add a little water if needed to take it up to the MAX line.

5 Blend until smooth.

CHEF'S NOTE

Flaxseeds are a rich source of micro-nutrients, dietary fibre, manganese, vitamin B1, and the essential fatty acid omega-3.

GRAPEFRUIT & APPLE JUICE

285 calories

Ingredients

- 50g/2oz spinach
- 1 apple
- 1 grapefruit
- 3 tbsp non fat Greek yogurt

- 120ml/½ cup unsweetened almond milk
- 5 chopped macadamia nuts
- Ice cubes
- Water

Method

1 Rinse and core the apple.

2 Peel and de-seed the grapefruit.

3 Add everything to the blender. Top up with ice cubes and water.

4 Make sure the ingredients do not go past the MAX line on your machine.

5 Blend until smooth.

CHEF'S NOTE
Grapefruit contains natural acids that cleanse the skin as well as vitamin C which acts as an antioxidant.

CHIA CINNAMON TOFU SMOOTHIE

330 calories

Ingredients

- 75g/3oz blueberries
- 1 banana
- 75g/3oz silken tofu
- 2 tsp chia seeds
- ½ tsp ground cinnamon
- 2 tsp honey
- 250ml/1 cup 1% milk
- Water

Method

1 Rinse the blueberries well. Peel the banana.

2 Add these to the blender along with all the other ingredients. Make sure they don't go past the MAX line on your machine.

3 Top up with water as far as the MAX line.

4 Blend until smooth.

CHEF'S NOTE
Cinnamon has been used throughout the ages to treat everything from a common cold to muscle spasms.

SPINACH & HEMP SMOOTHIE

345 calories

Ingredients

- 1 banana
- 50g/2oz spinach
- ½ ripe avocado
- 2 tbsp non fat Greek yogurt
- 1 tsp honey
- 2 tsp hemp seeds
- Water

Method

1 Peel the banana.

2 Rinse the spinach and remove any thick stalks.

3 Peel and stone the avocado.

4 Place all the ingredients in the blender, making sure they do not go past the MAX line on your machine.

5 Add a little water if needed to take it up to the MAX line.

6 Blend until smooth.

CHEF'S NOTE
Avocado and banana create a lovely thick base for this smoothie.

ALMOND PASSION SMOOTHIE

300 calories

Ingredients

- 200g/7oz mango
- 100g/3½oz passion fruit
- 2 tbsp fat-free Greek yogurt
- 25g/1oz spinach
- 250ml/1 cup unsweetened almond milk
- 50g/2oz silken tofu
- Water

Method

1 Peel, de-stone and cube the mango.

2 Halve the passion fruit and scoop out the flesh, adding it to the blender cup.

3 Add all the other ingredients. Make sure they do not go past the MAX line on your machine.

4 Add a little water if needed to take it up to the MAX line.

5 Blend until smooth.

CHEF'S NOTE
Try with flavoured Greek yogurt if you wish.

NUTTY SWEET POTATO SMOOTHIE

275 calories

Ingredients

- 50g/2oz spinach
- 150g/5oz sweet potato
- 250ml/1 cup unsweetened almond milk
- 1 tbsp almonds
- 1 scoop protein powder
- Water

Method

1 Rinse the ingredients well.

2 Remove any thick stalks from the spinach.

3 Cube the sweet potato, no need to peel if you have a very powerful blender.

4 Add the spinach, sweet potato, almond milk, almonds and protein powder to the blender. Make sure the ingredients do not go past the MAX line on your machine.

5 Add a little water if needed to take it up to the MAX line.

6 Blend until smooth.

CHEF'S NOTE
Sweet potatoes are an exceptionally rich source of vitamin A.

PROTEIN SCOOP SMOOTHIE

280 calories

Ingredients

- 2 tsp flax seeds
- 125g/4oz raspberries
- 1 scoop vanilla protein powder
- 250ml/1 cup 1% milk
- Ice cubes

Method

1 Rinse the raspberries.

2 Add all the ingredients to the blender making sure the ice does not go past the MAX line on your machine.

3 Blend until smooth.

CHEF'S NOTE
Flax seeds can help eliminate toxins from the body, regulate the metabolism and reduce blood sugar levels.

SALAD SPICE JUICE

300
calories

Ingredients

- 1 tomato
- 250ml/1 cup almond milk
- 1 stalk celery
- 1 small romaine lettuce
- ½ avocado

- 1 tbsp chopped fresh mint leaves
- 1 tsp ground ginger
- 1 pinch cayenne pepper
- Ice

Method

1 Rinse the ingredients well.

2 De-stone the avocado.

3 Add everything to the blender finishing with ice.

4 Make sure the ingredients do not go past the MAX line on your machine.

5 Blend until smooth.

CHEF'S NOTE
Ginger has a long history of use for treating nausea, motion sickness and pain.

PEAR & SOYA SMOOTHIE

295 calories

Ingredients

- 1 pear
- 1 banana
- 120ml/½ cup soya milk

- 2 tbsp non fat Greek yogurt
- 1 tbsp chopped walnuts
- 2 tsp flax seeds

Method

1 Rinse and core the pear.

2 Peel the banana and break into three.

3 Add all the ingredients to the blender.

4 Make sure the ingredients do not go past the MAX line on your machine.

5 Blend until smooth.

CHEF'S NOTE

Pears contain pectin that has a positive mild laxative effect on the body.

COCONUT & PINEAPPLE GREEN SMOOTHIE

245 calories

Ingredients

- 50g/2oz spinach
- 120ml/½ cup coconut water
- 120ml/½ cup 1% milk
- 1 banana

- 2 tbsp non fat Greek yogurt
- 75g/3oz fresh pineapple
- Water

Method

1 Rinse the spinach well and remove any thick stalks.

2 Peel the banana and break into three pieces. Peel the pineapple.

3 Add all the ingredients the to the blender. Make sure they do not go past the MAX line on your machine.

4 Add a little water if needed to take it up to the MAX line.

5 Blend until smooth.

CHEF'S NOTE
Use tinned pineapple if you don't have fresh pineapple to hand.

SMOOTH SUPER GREEN SMOOTHIE

380 calories

Ingredients

- 50g/2oz kale
- 50g/1oz spinach
- ½ avocado
- 1 tsp honey

- 1 apple
- 3 tbsp non fat Greek yogurt
- 1 tbsp ground almonds
- Ice cubes

Method

1 Wash the kale & spinach. Cut any thick stems off the kale.

2 Peel and de-stone the avocado. Core the apple.

3 Place everything in the blender . Make sure the ingredients do not go past the MAX line on your machine.

4 Add a little water if needed.

5 Blend until smooth.

CHEF'S NOTE
Kale is nutrient-rich and contains zero fat.

BROCCOLI & CHIA SEED SMOOTHIE

297 calories

Ingredients

- 50g/2oz tenderstem broccoli
- 1 apple
- 1 banana
- 1 tbsp chia seeds

- 250ml/1 cup soya milk
- 1 scoop protein powder
- Water

Method

1 Rinse the ingredients well.

2 Core the apple and peel the banana.

3 Add all the ingredients to the blender. Make sure the ingredients do not go past the MAX line on your machine.

4 Add water, again being careful not to exceed the MAX line.

5 Blend until smooth.

CHEF'S NOTE
Chia seeds are nutrient dense and pack a serious energy punch.

COCONUT & OAT SMOOTHIE

360 calories

Ingredients

FIBRE RICH

- 1 scoop protein powder
- 1 tbsp coconut cream
- 250ml/1 cup oat milk
- 1 banana
- Water

Method

1 Peel the banana.

2 Add all the ingredients to the blender.

3 Make sure the ingredients do not go past the MAX line on your machine.

4 Add a little water if needed to take it up to the MAX line.

5 Blend until smooth.

CHEF'S NOTE
Soya or 1% milk make good alternatives to oat milk.

SPRING TIME SMOOTHIE

278 calories

Ingredients

- 75g/3oz shredded spring cabbage greens
- 1 banana
- 250ml/1 cup soya milk
- 1 scoop potein powder
- 2 tsp honey
- 1 tbsp pumpkin seeds
- Water

Method

1 Rinse the ingredients well.

2 Peel the banana.

3 Add the greens, fruit, nuts & milk to the blender. Make sure the ingredients do not go past the MAX line on your machine.

4 Add water, again being careful not to exceed the MAX line.

5 Blend until smooth.

CHEF'S NOTE

Spring greens are the first cabbages of the year. They have loose heads without the tough core of other cabbages.